Stop S

STOP SETTLING, SIS... JUST WAIT FOR MR. RIGHT

Also by Demetria Davis

A Child Scorned, A Woman Reborn

STOP SETTLING, SIS... JUST WAIT FOR MR. RIGHT

BY: DEMETRIA DAVIS

Published by Pen 2 Pen Publishing
Est. 2012

Pen 2 Pen Publishing
2261 Talmadge Rd.
Suite #71
Lovejoy, GA 30250

ISBN:
Printed in the U.S.A.

Email: info@pen2penpublishing.com

Table of Contents

Introduction

What were we thinking? Have you ever taken a glimpse back over your life, at all the bad relationships, all the mistakes you made, and the men you settled for? Did you come across Mr. Counterfeit while waiting for Mr. Right? Of course you have!

Let me ask again. What were we thinking?

This book is designed to shed some light into the lives of women all over the world who may be asking themselves: What did I do? Where did I go wrong? Why me? This book will help you get to the next level in your life with confidence that your Mr. Right is on the way, so you'll never have to settle again!

Now is not the time for women to figure out what it takes to attract good Godly men. It's time for us to figure out what it takes for us to Love ourselves enough to receive. **Genesis 2:18 (NLT)** says: *"Then the Lord said, 'It is not good for the man to be alone. I will make a helper who is just right for him.'"*

God knew there would be a great need for the woman to be in a man's life, so therefore we were created. **(Genesis 2:22)** God has gifted, challenged yet strengthened us to endure many battles, but there's one fight I truly believe belongs to the Lord, and that is how to, "Stop Settling Sis... and just wait for Mr. Right."

There have been countless times that I, myself, have gone down the same road, doing the same things, but praying for different results. I was going about the dating process without including God. Which reminds me of this quote: "If you want something different, you have to do something different."

What is the first thing we need to learn to do different that will keep us from settling? We have to learn to value ourselves more! We have to begin looking at ourselves the way God already sees us. Come on, say it with me "I am fearfully and wonderfully made!" According to **Psalms 139:14 (KJV)** this also means No More Settling! If the way you see yourself has been the reason you have settled in the past, here is where you do something different.

I had to wake up and realize, "I am Beautiful!" I will no longer settle for the abuse that comes with settling for Mr. Wrong and neither will you.

I was truly inspired to write this book after dating the "bad timing guy." You know, the guy that's always willing to see you, but always at the wrong time? That's the bad timing guy! Let me give you an example:

If our plans were to go on our date at 7:30, he would say:

"I can't make it by that time. Is 8:30 okay?"
When 8:30 would come around he would say:
"I'm going to be a little late. Is that okay?"
Would you like to know what I said?
"No, it's not okay!"

It appeared to me that if he was unable to keep the first time he would surely make it for the second one, but he failed twice. You may be saying that was so simple, but let's think for a minute, Ladies. If we have to train ourselves how to be good women, very approachable, loving, caring and forgiving, the least they can learn to do is be prompt.

Know what you want out of a relationship. If you allow little things that you know you don't like to slip past you in the beginning of the relationship, there is certainly no chance in believing you can change something you have already accepted. My motto is this: "At the end of the day, all a man has left is his word, and he should always keep it."

I had dated men and settled for them in numerous ways, some I am almost ashamed to share. However, I will because I know I am not the only one. There are so many women that need to know they can do better and be healed by just reading this very book. I came up with a chart that I will share with you later on in this introductory section that will give you a closer look at some of the things that you may have settled for in men.

After questioning myself over and over again as to why relationships weren't working out, it was as if God himself woke up my spirit and said, "Stop settling...Just wait for Mr. Right." I had to realize that I am a Virtuous Woman and remind myself of God's Word. This brought two scriptures to my memory.

Proverbs 31:10 (KJV) reads: *"Who can find a Virtuous Woman? For her price is far above rubies."* *Keywords* Far Above! This means the value of my Virtue had just gone up! Amen!

He also reminded me of what **Proverbs 18:22 (KJV)** says: *"Whoso findeth a wife findeth a good thing, and obtaineth favor from the Lord."* Which means when God adds value to your life you become as a treasure holding precious jewels. It has then been left up to the man to seek out the most hidden stones in order to obtain favor from the Lord.

But how can you be found if you're not hidden?

Here is my theory: A single Christian Lady (who believes in the Lord Jesus Christ as your Savior) or any lady for that matter should not be "everywhere all the time." Learning not to settle means making yourself conveniently unavailable sometimes. You just cannot be at every party, every gathering, and every ladies' night outing just because you received an invitation. It's okay to want to be noticed. Otherwise, how will you ever be found? However you have to learn to make some sacrifices at times. Your flesh is desperate to break loose. It's called dying daily, but we will get into that later in the book.

So what does it mean to settle? Let's define it. Settling is to become satisfied with or in a situation that is lower or beneath ones ideal living standards. Whoa! I don't know about you, but when I first read this I was blown away! I do not feel any woman or man should belittle themselves to this level. It's simply not worth it. It is more beneficial to do as the saying goes: "I can do bad all by myself." Until God sends the right man along. And he will.

This is the portion of the book to be honest with yourself. It will help you to learn from and gain healing from the mistakes that we've made so that we can "Stop settling and just wait for Mr. Right."

Let's make a list of the settlements. We will call these the Settle 4's. On one side you will see some of the things we have settled for. On the other side, you will see some of the excuses we use to continue settling. This is a psychological assessment or psychological test which is utilized to assess the performance of an individual. It also helps with identifying strengths and weaknesses. Scores are tallied and determined based upon the individual's sincere and conscientious response. So please be honest with yourself!

SETTLE4'S

(5)	Not Saved	But People can change
(9)	Has no car	It was wrecked or Repo'd
(10)	Borrows your money	He will pay me back
(6)	Has four or more kids	He takes care of them
(10)	Has no money	He is in between jobs
(10)	No Job	He is a hustler
(8)	Lives with his Mom	He's going through hard times
(10)	Physically Abusive	He still loves me
(5)	Never calls, only text	He is busy a lot
(7)	Bad timing	There's always tomorrow
(10)	Borrows your car	He puts gas in the tank
(9)	Never Compliments you	I know how he feels
(8)	Jealous	He just wants me to himself
(10)	Verbally abusive	He don't mean no harm
(10)	Drug User	He's going through something
(9)	Womanizer	He comes home every night
(7)	No vision for the future	He talks but doesn't deliver

Right in front of the Settle4's you will see a number. I want you to write on a separate sheet of paper the number for each one of these Settle4's listed above that you have settled for. What was the outcome of your list? If you checked five or more, or you scored 50 or higher, "It's Time to Stop Settling and Just Wait for Mr. Right!"

Once you realize you have put yourself in a situation and compromised your self-worth for someone that did not reciprocate the same qualities as you, it is then time to reevaluate your standards. But never belittle yourself or feel like you are unworthy of meeting someone great because you have come across someone that didn't have good qualities. We are only human, and we all make mistakes. Trust me, bad things happen to good people, so this type of behavior has the ability to fall upon even the best of us. It is getting past these cycles of events that define who we are and how we will entertain future relationships.

It is necessary to do a self-evaluation of your emotions after coming out of a bad relationship. We must make sure that after coming out of relationships that have left us broken that we have the ability to be mended. We also must take the time to heal. If we do not go through the process of healing, we eventually become bitter, and when bitterness sets in it then becomes very hard to be an effective person for potential relationships.

Recognize where you have gone wrong in previous relationships. We cannot always put the blame on the other person just because things did not work out. Ask yourself, what are some of the things that you may need to change? Do you need to become a better person? Do you need to be a little more humble with people? Are there things you could have said and done to gain more understanding in the relationship? Do you need to change the way you think?

These are all helpful questions that will give you positive results and should help you build your self- esteem. Get to know yourself first. Concentrate on some of the things you like. Get to know yourself inside and out. There may be some hidden characteristics down in you that you were not aware of. Find out what truly makes you happy. What can you do to make someone else happy? What are your deal breakers in relationships? What makes you go off the deep end?

Once you find out more about yourself, you will begin to focus more on what can be done in order to make relationships work in your future. Life, love, and happiness is always about being true to yourself, but in order to do that you have to learn to forgive yourself of your mistakes. The next few chapters of this book will not only teach you how to forgive yourself but also how to love yourself even more. It will teach you step by step how to start a process of events that will help you become a better you, which will keep you from settling for Mr. Wrong.

As we move forward to Chapter 1 it will help you to reflect on how controlling the way we think can help us to stop settling for people who don't deserve us and how to become more attracted to Greatness.

CHAPTER ONE

Control Your Thoughts

Thinking is inevitable. It's impossible to have a waking day and not have various thoughts run through our minds. Have you ever made a promise to yourself and had to fight with your mind to keep that promise? Making promises to ourselves can be a rather difficult task, especially if we're promising to do something in an area we are the most weak. I found this to be true because I failed at the promise I made to myself over and over again.

One thing we should know is that our mind is very powerful, having the ability to reason, think, feel, perceive, judge, and store massive amounts of memory on a daily basis. Isn't it amazing how your mind can go back and conjure up things from your past you thought you had forgotten?

Which brings me to this point, if your mind has the power to do that, it ultimately has the power to take control over any matter, situation, or circumstance. If you're like me you may be saying or thinking right now, *but every time I try to think the right thoughts, a negative thought will try to intervene.* This is what's called battle of the mind.

When you begin to battle in your mind between the good things that your mind notes and the bad things your mind contradict, it can be very hard to keep a promise that you made to yourself. Trust me, I know the feeling of wavering between what's good and what's bad. So when I begin having doubts about my own thoughts, I begin to go to the Creator of all my thoughts, our Heavenly Father.

There is a scripture in **Philippians 2:5** (KJV) that reads: *"Let this mind be in you that was also in Christ Jesus."* What a wonderful world this would be if we all could learn to operate in the likeness of Jesus! However, because we are flesh and the Word is spirit, we must use the word as our guide when our thoughts are thrown off track. Believe it or not our mind and the way we think have a lot to do with why we settle for Mr. Wrong.

Utilizing God's word and having the mind of Christ is what helps us to stay focused on the promises we have made to ourselves. We should always question our thoughts. *Was that a good thought*? Or if a thought came to mind that didn't appear to be fruitful or beneficial to the situation you're dealing with, simply ask yourself, *"Was that a righteous (or right) way of thinking?"*

I have had to ask myself that very question. And there have certainly been thoughts contrary to Godly thinking that arose in me, but I still did what "I" wanted to do. Why? Because I was having a problem developing my thoughts which should've been centered on God's word.

We must understand that all of our thoughts originate from the Creator of life; however they can be tampered with by the enemy or the "Inner-Me," which is ourselves with our stinking and distorted thinking. So unless we are willing to get free from the turmoil of battling with the thoughts in our mind, we will always break the promises we make to ourselves. Breaking our own promises we make to ourselves leads to self-destruction and defeat. *"For though we walk in the flesh, we do not war after the flesh. For the weapons of our warfare are not carnal, but mighty through God to the pulling down of strongholds. Casting down imaginations and every high thing that exalteth itself against the obedience of Christ.*" **2 Corinthians 10: 3-5 (KJV)**

This scripture clearly means, in learning how to deal with our thoughts we must first recognize that they are carnal (flesh). Although we are human fleshly beings, we must not walk according to the way flesh would lead us, which is the way of the world. God has given us something far better than fleshly/worldly power. What he has given us is divine and spiritual. His authority has given us the power to break the chain of anything that tries to hold our thoughts captive.

Please allow me to give you an example.

Let's say there is a rumor going on about you on your job. Something that you know is not true. What do you do? Your MIND would probably tell you to improvise a plan to defend your innocence without realizing you have defeated yourself. One thing about our truth is, it's always true. So when a lie challenges it, instead of avoiding the battle that comes with trying to figure out why the rumor started, our mind tells us to figure it out. To question it, to get to the bottom of it. Because that's what an uncontrolled mind does. It wants and *has* to know why. It only operates in rationale and has to have the reason why things happen. However, when we learn how to control our thoughts, our mind doesn't need an explanation for untruth.

2 Corinthians 10:5 reminds us that God himself gives us the power to cast down every vain thought, imagination, or lie that false accusers bring upon us. Allowing your spirit to control your thoughts will always give you the best result. However keep in mind God will never try to stop or control our way of thinking. Never! I've heard people say, *"Lord, change the way I think."* But it just doesn't work like that. Even David recognized he was a sinful man, so his prayer was, *"Create in me a clean heart, O God; and renew a right spirit within me."* **(Psalms 51:10**

KJV) He did not ask the Lord to change the way he thinks; he asked to be cleaned up and renewed, meaning, give me a second chance so that next time I may choose wisely. That's why God gives us choices and allows us to make our own decisions based upon our level of maturity. This comes in time as we coach and train our minds to think on a higher level in him and not ourselves. I like to call this the "out of the box way of thinking."

When learning how to control our thoughts we must recognize our problem area. What is it that makes me do the things I do, say the things I say, or act the ways I act. We cannot be a surface thinker when it comes to controlling our thoughts. We must be able to see things from different angles, points of view, and sometimes by the opinion of others. Do not always assume that the way you are thinking is the only way things are. Search for new methods of learning and always remain open to education. Gleaning from positive individuals can also be very essential for mental growth and development. It's all about keeping negative thoughts from bombarding your mind. If you do so you are almost guaranteed to think clearly.

Now that we have covered the importance of how to control our thoughts, let's go back to keeping the promises we make to ourselves. Remember I said it's always harder to keep a promise in the area that you're most weak in? So that means you have to try extremely hard to stay focused on your words.

Example: if a person has promised they would go on a diet, then as a result of this, they cannot eat their favorite snack, which is cookies. Can you imagine how hard it can be to keep that promise with temptation all around you? That person could've just stepped off the treadmill and someone walks over with a bag of cookies and offers to share. This is where the mind/spirit has to be stronger than the flesh/carnality.

In the book of **Matthew 26:41 (KJV)** it says: *"Watch and pray, that ye enter not into temptation; the spirit is indeed willing but the flesh is weak."*

We have to pray in times of promises because we not only make the promise unto ourselves, but unto the Lord through the spirit which he hears through our thoughts. So why did Jesus say to the disciples in verse 41 above, *"the spirit is indeed willing but the flesh is weak?"* Jesus knew that when we are in a state of contentment and happiness, we make decisions predicated upon our emotions. Happy people make happy decisions and sad people make fleshly decisions when their faith is tempted. This means we will allow our spirit to make promises in our happier moments that our flesh cannot keep when we are sad and vulnerable. It is easier for the enemy to send cunning things your way when you are sad and vulnerable, or the "inner me" to allow them to come in. (Like a handsome man that does not have good intentions for your life.) That is why it is very important to have the mind of Christ and no matter what the devil sends your way you have to be able to stand on God's word which says: "Stand still and know that I am God" Psalms 46:10 (KJV)

We have to be careful of what we entertain when trying to focus on keeping the promises we make to ourselves. The number one thing that we have to be mindful of is entertaining "Mr. Wrong."

What are our thoughts of Love and relationship? I'm sure that we all, as women, have experienced a "love encounter" or what we thought was an authentic love encounter that turned out to be something far different than we'd hoped or dreamed of.

Before I got married I can remember going through a cycle of defeat in love. It appeared that I was either attracting the wrong men or I was too vulnerable to wait for Mr. Right. Unconsciously, I was thinking that I was going about relationships the right way. The typical behavior was formulaic.

Man shows interest... if he's attractive enough then engage with him... set up a date... go out a few times... become intimate, then from like to love...or was it lust? Great question right?

Now, your experience with failed relationships may have been different from mine, and although mine varied in how we approached a commitment or whether there was ever an official commitment or not, they still did not land in marriage. However, I was always left wondering what I did wrong and questioning the reason why neither of them were Mr. Right.

Well, I can tell you what I was doing wrong. I was not valuing myself enough. I did not know my worth. I did not know what it meant to wait for Mr. Right because I was unable to identify with him. The way I *thought* about relationships as opposed to the way I *felt* in relationships didn't add up.

My thoughts of righteousness or "right living" were all scrambled. My mind knew the right thing to do, but my heart wasn't allowing it. I began to battle with my need to wait on God and the thought of, "this may be the one."

There were several times I thought to myself, *this is not right, this can't be the will of God because if so, it would feel different.*

But time and time again what I thought was right would hit a rough patch and end just as quickly as it had started. See, when our mind is battling with our emotions it's clear that thoughts can be a bit wavered.

As women we generally go into situations thinking with our hearts and feeling with our minds. I know you may say that seems backward and that would be true, but that's typically our route. We do not begin to think rationally and logically until we are already head over heels in a situation and our thoughts are begging to be realigned.

So, that begs to ask the question: how do we realign our thoughts? Realigning our thoughts is simply learning how to control our thoughts so that you begin to think of better things. Thinking of better things is equivalent to having faith that better things are to come. Here's a small list of things to consider when realigning and controlling your thoughts for better things

1. Love yourself first
2. Change your perspective
3. Believe that you deserve better
4. Treat yourself kindly
5. Be observant yet optimistic
6.   Make a deal breaker list
7. Be okay with saying No
8. Take your time
9. Develop a friendship
10. Date for marriage

Controlling the thoughts of how you view yourself allows others to view you in the same regard. Loving oneself is the most powerful weapon that one can carry. Have you ever noticed that there are some people you've viewed and wondered how they got a husband? I can reassure you it is because they knew what it took for them to attract the person that they loved which was/is self, first. The thought of what will it take or what should I do to attract Mr. Right should be shifted to what should I do for myself. Believing in yourself is also a thought which we will discuss in chapter two. Trust me when I say this, no one on the face of this earth is going to treat you better than you, so learn to treat yourself kindly which will cause a mirror effect when you meet a man.

Learn to be observant. What are your thoughts telling you about the person that could be your potential Mr. Right? Are there things that you noticed according to the Settle 4's mentioned in the introduction that you think will just not work for you? If so, know that it's okay to make that deal breaker list. Otherwise, you may settle for something you do not want. It's okay to turn down the first offer. Saying no sets the tone and the standard. There are plenty of fish in the sea, but you don't have to put the first one in the bucket just because he came flapping out of the water. Have patience; take your time with your selection. Utilize your new frame of mind to attract the right one. Focus on controlling your thoughts so much so that you can feel it when it's right.

Last but not least develop a friendship. Get to know your person of interest. Don't make the mistake I made so many times of thinking I knew the person but was only aware of what was visible on the surface. Ask questions about their past, see if they are the type of person that has good relationships with family as well as others. Go out together, be curious about what their public and private life looks like. Do they introduce you to other friends? If so, find out what other friends are saying about them. The key to knowing if you have attracted a good suitor is to let them know from the beginning that you are dating for marriage. If you do not get past the friendship/dating phase once this is announced, Mr. Wrong will run. Only if he sees something in you that is worth sticking around for will Mr. Right stay.

Now that we've learned how to control our thoughts, we're on our way!

CHAPTER TWO

Believe In Yourself

Believing in you is simple. Just say, "I can do this" and that settles it. **Philippians 4:13 (KJV)** says, *"I can do all things through Christ that strengthens me."* Your very own thoughts create words, and your words have the power to create Life and Victory or defeat and death. The choice is yours. **Proverbs 18:21(KJV)** says Death and Life are in the power of the tongue. We should always be careful how we use our words towards our life, family, finances, marriages, children and also our church. We are held accountable for every word that proceeds from our tongue, therefore we should learn to use speech wisely.

The way you see your life should not be the way you view your life. To see your life is to look at it from its present tense, meaning, when I open my eyes I see everything around me that is happening now. But if you begin to view your life, that means you are picturing things that are happening from afar. A dictionary term used for view means: *To take aim with intention or purpose.*

Now ask yourself, what does it mean to take aim with intention and purpose? It means to view your life as it could be, with plans to fulfill the will of God. Or let us use the term to have a Bird's Eye View.

An Eagle's vision is about five times sharper than the human eye sight. So the Eagle has the ability to see things that are far off. In other words, the bird never goes after something that is directly in sight; he views his target from a distance before he decides to go after it. Now if the Eagle did not take aim with intention and purpose before attempting to conquer its goal, the Eagle would have failed. Why am I saying this? Because when we're only seeing life in its present tense but attempting to obtain a better future without first viewing the bigger picture, we fail.

Therefore, we must train ourselves to believe in ourselves. If what you are seeing in your current situation is not the results you would like to see in your life, I challenge you to view it from the Bird's Eye View. View your life from a higher level of living. It's okay to dream, but when you dream, dream Big! It's all about the things that you believe in that you will achieve in. We have to move out of the realm of small-minded thinking. We have trapped ourselves for so long with mediocre lifestyles until we have become comfortable with only having just enough. We must knock down the wall in our minds that block us from getting to our greater living.

A greater life is possible for all who believe. I don't care what your current situation is right now, and neither should you. Instead, focus on the things God has for your future. What do you see? If you do not have a vision of a better future you will remain stuck in your present condition. Believe it or not, allowing your mind to stay in a state of complacency is where Mr. Wrong will always find you. Why is it so easy for Mr. Wrong to find you in that place? Because you don't have enough faith to believe that your future can get better. God is always waiting to open new doors for his children, but we have to build that relationship with him and begin to trust and believe that he wants us to live a great life. Which would you rather do, remain complacent or allow Mr. Right to find you in your great place? You do not have to wait on someone that is doing great to save you from your current place! Always attempt to find your greater purpose for your greater life.

I can remember having my first job when I was only 14 years old. I worked at a local restaurant. Although I was happy to have the job, even at that age I was not content. God had spoken to me after a series of events that took place and said, *"You will own businesses."* I heard this in my spirit just as clearly as you're reading this book. I was only a kid so quite naturally I did not know what it meant or what the future held, but from that moment forward I held on to those words the Lord gave me. I was living in public housing apartments so my living status at that time was very contrary to someone owning their own businesses. But it was something deep down on the inside of me that challenged me to believe that God could change that. I was open and willing to allow God to change everything about the way my current situation appeared by focusing on what I wanted my future to look like. I believed that I could accomplish anything. Now that may sound crazy to you but it's true. I had also placed certain things in my life that did not exist yet. Yes I did those things; I even knew what type of cars I wanted to drive in my future. After going through all the hardship I had endured, I knew that I wanted a life of luxury and I would have to believe in it by faith until it came to pass. What other way was there? There is a such thing as miracles, and yes they do happen, but even in receiving a miracle you must get up every day with an expectant heart.

You MUST BEGIN TO FOCUS ON WHAT YOU WANT FOR YOUR LIFE and focus on what it takes to receive it. Remember, Faith without works is dead, so you must not think that you can get up every day and say I'm going to be a millionaire without any action. What efforts are you putting forth in order to achieve this goal? There are great things out there waiting for all of us; however I would be lying to you if I told you that you could receive God's gifts and blessings without first working for it. Receiving something from God is like working a nine to five job and receiving your paycheck every week. Because you earned it you received it. However, the work that we do to receive our blessings from God are simple. Have faith, then get up and put that faith into action.

Your payout for having "faith" causes us to receive certain benefits that will help make life easier. This is how it works with the Father. If you have a desire to have wonderful things in your life you should show God by working towards it. How do you do that? By reaching out to him, trusting, leaning, and depending on him. He is the source of your supply.

He said in his word, *"For every beast of the forest is mine, the cattle on a thousand hills."* **Psalms 50:10 (KJV)** That means if everything is his then who should you ask for your blessings? That's right, God! It does not matter what you have need of or how impossible it may seem, we serve a God that specializes in the impossible. Believing in yourself is dreaming big unless you don't love or have faith in yourself. What other way is there to dream? No one should dream to be more broke every time they wake up. If so, the enemy or "inner me" is playing tricks with your mind and you should revisit Chapter One. On the flip side, if you are expecting God to do some big things in your life, TRUST HIM!

With that being said, let's say you drive a Honda but have dreams of owning a Mercedes. You have to dream big! If you live in a Townhouse but have dreams of owning your own Mansion, you have to dream big! You may be settling for Mr. Wrong right now and want to be blessed with Mr. Right... you have to dream big! You may have dreams of going from employee to Business Owner/CEO...YOU HAVE TO DREAM BIG!

Say this with me: "I will not only speak these things over my life but I will also conquer all these areas of my life. Not because I'm so good at everything that I have done but because I believe in myself. I will begin to speak things over my life into the atmosphere."

If you recite this affirmation every day, you will see a change in things. Your perspective will change and your life will begin to change because of it.

Here is the key that unlocks your dreams. Let's define it.

What is belief? It is an acceptance that a statement is true or that something exists; something that one accepts as being true or real, which is their own firmly held opinion.

Now, isn't that deep! That means you have to stand by what you believe in no matter what! If God says you can have it, that means you speak it, you believe it, and it shall come to pass. Things do not manifest themselves off thoughts alone. No Ma'am! You have to speak them into existence. There is absolutely no reason for anyone to covet, envy, or be jealous of what another person has. God has given us all the power we need to benefit from this universe. So the same thing someone else accomplishes you can too by what you speak. Don't be held back any longer by worrying about what "sister so and so" has! Believe in yourself! The Bible says in **Matthew 21:22 (NLT)** *"You can pray for anything and if you have Faith you can receive it."* That does not mean start praying that your enemies fall dead and believe in it so hard that it happens. If you do that, then you're serving a false God. I do not believe our God blesses evil prayers. God will even use your enemies oftentimes to bless you and keep you focused. So, he does not want us to bicker about others, hate one another or try to manipulate each other to make it to the top. He simply wants us to trust him and believe in ourselves.

Please do not get the false impression that if you want something, just because a Pastor stands in the pulpit and says it's your season that it's going to happen overnight. We must understand that God will use men and women to speak something into our lives what he may have already shown you, therefore it becomes confirmation. However you still have to be steadfast, unmovable, and always abounding in him. Remember you are trusting in God and believing in yourself, so you do not want to get so caught up in having a husband that you become delusional. You want to always remain in control of your thoughts by being able to distinguish the difference between desperate by flesh and patient by the spirit.

Being patient has always proven to produce better fruit. Think of it this way, everything has its season. Fruits and vegetables have to be planted at a certain time of the year. Once they have been planted the earth has to become saturated with water to start the process of growth. After the process has begun, the fruits and vegetables begin to grow. However, they will not become ripe until their set timing. Now the farmer can choose to pick the fruits or veggies from their maturation stage before they have completely developed, but he will have an incomplete product. Plucking an incomplete product before its opportune time of development will always lead to the spoil of goods. So the product then becomes damaged in less than the time that it took to plant it.

In other words, if you be patient and trust God, he will send you your mate. I truly believe that not only will he send your mate but he will send him right on time. It will be your season to reap what you have sown. The Father is a timely God; he knows when to plant, he knows when to water, and he knows when to pluck. His timing is perfect. And this is what we have to believe.

Trust that God is not only preparing your mate for you to receive in your set timing (season), but know also that he is preparing you. Let him begin the process in your life. If you are not planted in a Ministry, by all means let the Lord speak to you, lead you and guide you to a place where your spirit can be watered. If Church is not your preference for whatever your reason, by all means try involving your spirit in his word. The Word of God will begin to heal you from the inside out. It is very important that you begin to believe that God can do the impossible when you become planted. You will then begin to grow in the things of God. He will begin to erase all of the negative things that tried to hold you back from believing in yourself. Let God have his way in your life. Don't get discouraged or dismayed over your circumstances or situations that may arise, just stay planted. Build your relationship with God with the understanding that you are being developed and matured and that you shall not be moved.

Pray and ask God what your assignment will be, and what he would have for you to do within the Ministry. If your Spirituality does not take you within the four walls of the Church, there's no pressure, quietly seek God wherever you choose but by all means, seek him for guidance and clarity. Focus while you wait on Mr. Right because he's out there but God needs to get you in a place of preparation and maturation just as he does with the fruits and vegetables. Be careful not to uproot yourself where you feel God is watering you for growth. The enemy or "inner me" can be cunning and will make you feel like the thing that you are believing, hoping and praising God for will never come and what happens often times is we remove ourselves from our blessed place before the blessing comes. This will cause us to become an incomplete product and we then become damaged goods.

Utilize your time getting to know God for yourself from the inside out. Form a relationship with him that is so solid that he becomes your number one focus. He will begin to purge and cleanse you of all the memories that haunt you, bad habits and mistakes while ordering and preparing your steps. He will mold and develop you into the woman you have been chosen to be.

2 Timothy 2:21 (NLT) reads: *"If you keep yourself pure, you will be a special utensil for honorable use. Your life will be clean, and you will be ready for the Master to use you for every good work."*

You can do this! Believe In Yourself!

CHAPTER THREE

The Celebration of Being Single

Go ahead and ask me...how do I celebrate being Single? Easy! But you may feel like being single is a very hard to deal with.

First things first, do not let being single mess up your mind. The first thing we must keep in mind is when you are a lover of God you are never alone! To be single does not mean desperate, and to be alone does not mean lonely. Believe it or not being single is a peaceful place. God has a way of doing everything. He gives us supplemental things to fill the voids in our lives until we are ready for our mate. And during the preparation process he is always there.

His word says in **Hebrew 13:5 (KJV)** *"Let your conversation be without covetousness and be content with such things as ye have for he hath said; I will never leave thee nor forsake thee."*

In other words, do not hold conversations about having what another woman has, such as her husband, her job, children, car or anything else that she has been blessed with. Instead, be content with things you already have. God is ready to bless you with the things he has planned for your life and nobody else's.

Would you believe me if I told you God already has blessings with your name on them? It belongs to you. He is waiting on the most important thing from each of us as it relates to receiving our blessing. He simply wants us to ask for them. He has promised that if we have faith and believe, we are then able to receive. Even during the midst of the wait he also promised to never leave us nor forsake us. So even in the times we feel all alone we are able to take him at his word and know that he is there.

Now, the first great way to celebrate being single is to love you! Yes, I said it: Love *you* first. It is nobody's responsibility to love someone that does not find them self-loveable.

Could you imagine how hard it would be for Mr. Right to love the woman that feels she's Mrs. Wrong?

No one wants to deal with someone who is always complaining about themselves. I understand there may be some things that you may not feel comfortable with about yourself; so it is perfectly normal to identify with them. However, there is always room for improvement.

Please allow me to guide you on how to start your day and explain some of the things it took for me to stop settling.

Let's start by beginning the day with some nice relaxing music. Listen to the kind of music that tranquilizes all senses and calms all nerves. The kind of music that takes you away from anything that has been troubling you. Music that just allows you to unwind. If you are a gospel lover play some nice worship music. Or perhaps you may be into contemporary jazz, neo soul, or smooth old school R & B. No matter what the preference of melody you choose, make sure it will help you to feel at ease. (Rap music will not help you, in this case.) Try to create an environment that is conducive to relaxation. It's always good to listen to something you like because before you know it you will be caught up with singing, dancing, praising, worshipping, loving and enjoying being YOU!

Next, take the time to run yourself a steamy aroma therapeutic bubble bath. Aromatherapy is a very good approach to relaxation and meditation. The wonderful fragrances help to alter the mood and behavior which will also benefit in the need for relaxation. Let's also light a couple candles around the tub. Candles are important when winding down because they give you a sense of peace, love and romance. It is important that we all learn how to bring our mind, body, soul, and spirit to a place where there is absolutely nothing but self-harmony. Remember, it's all about celebrating being single and loving you.

Now you must do this on a day when there is no hurry. You're just simply taking the time to love on you. I personally like to bring my laptop or iPad along with me. I choose to go on YouTube and watch a good ole sermon by either of my favorite preachers, Bishop Paul S. Morton, (which is my Pastor) being one of them, or other preferences. Your selection is totally up to you.

Receiving the word of God has always been a great way for me to loosen up and relax, so I would also use this time to give thanks unto God for his preparation of my day. I would begin to thank him in advance for all of the good things that were about to unfold for me. You have the power to control the outcome of your day by what you put into the atmosphere. So during this moment of worship, peace, and relaxation, speak out with a clear voice, "Today will be a great day!"

God said in his word that he will give us the peace that surpasses all understanding and will keep our hearts and mind through his son Christ Jesus. **Philippians 4:7 (KJV)**

By all means, do whatever the spirit of God leads you to do during your moment of isolation. You may simply want to be quiet, and that is perfectly fine. Let him purify you with his presence, no matter what your choice is. He will be with you. Command your day to be a peaceful day and no matter what tries to hinder that, it will not happen because you have the power to control your day. Once you have found the peace you need through your relaxation it is then time to move on to the next step... "THE MAKEOVER"

Okay ladies if you have not already purchased beauty products such as foundation make-up, eye shadows, liners, blush, and gloss, now is the time! Give yourself a make-over TODAY! I know some of you may be saying, "But I don't wear make-up I am an all-natural woman." I'm sure if you purchased this book you are an all-natural single woman or a woman that's settling in a relationship who could use a change. Every woman has room to experience new things, but only if she is willing to accept a little change into her life. What one man doesn't like or accept, trust me, another man will. So there is absolutely nothing wrong with wanting to be an "enhanced" beauty in order to attract Mr. Right. Make-up is a very nice enhancement for women; however we must learn how to apply it in moderation. And you can do this alone. It does not take 20 pounds of make-up to enhance our beauty, and it does not cost you anything to love yourself. Remember, practice makes perfect. Now, CATER TO YOU!

Walk up to the mirror and say, "I AM BEAUTIFUL!" This is the first thing you have to "know and believe" if you never want to settle for Mr. Wrong again. You have to realize that no matter what shape, size, race or complexion you may be "YOU ARE BEAUTIFUL!" We are all made in the image of God. **Genesis 1:27 (KJV)** God said it and we can believe it!

Women are a creation that is to be desired and appreciated so we should carry ourselves as such. So, without further ado, let's begin!

Start by picking colors for yourself that you feel are going to be suitable for your exciting day ahead. Once you have listened to wonderful music, relaxed with aromatherapy, and given thanks unto God for this day, your mood should be set. What color did you pick based upon your joyous mood? Perhaps something that will blend in perfectly with the classy attire you have chosen for yourself. Now if you have absolutely no experience applying make-up (beating your face) you can also go to a YouTube channel to watch online tutorials. YouTube videos can help with style and precision.

I am all things beauty by profession. Licensed as a Master Cosmetologist, so it is a pleasure to make women look and feel good about themselves. I do vending events all over the country in several states and when women approach my table but are unsure about the final look, I tell them the same thing. Your eyebrows, alone, speak volumes to the face. They can be boring and undone, they can say a lot when overly enhanced, or they can say just enough when done correctly. Oftentimes women only need a nice clean, contoured and concealed brow for the face to pop! The eyebrows alone will give the face a glow that makes everything else shine! Adding lashes, eye color, foundation and the lip are the bonuses! Once your facial beauty has been enhanced, take another look, smile and then GET DRESSED!

First things first, let's keep in mind you are Celebrating Being Single and loving you, so your attire should have nothing to do with who you will see today. The outfit you choose for today should speak deeply about your inner beauty. Let's think back for just a moment about controlling our thoughts, it's important to keep your mind frame centered on the fact that you are doing this for you. So even if you know you are feeling good and looking hot, let's not go about this makeover day with the intention of drawing attention. The focus here is to earnestly practice self-love. So let's not wear anything that's too revealing for men to see what should be covered. Concentrate and focus your thoughts on the right things, things that are going to attract Mr. Right and not Mr. Wrong.

For so many years I struggled with really loving myself so I thought that dressing a certain way was going to attract me a husband. WRONG! I had to learn how to control my thoughts and the way I viewed myself in order to believe I deserved the best. Let's not get it twisted. I love fashion, so there is absolutely nothing wrong with looking cute. However, I had to learn how to look cute but keep it Classy. If by any chance you are reading this book and it helps you to understand that there is a great need for you to change the way you dress, do not feel bad. I've been through the process. I have not written anything in this book that I have not personally experienced. If the truth should be told I was inspired to write this based upon my very own failures.

I realized that a lot of things I went through while choosing the wrong men was not all their fault. The blame was my very own. A man, whether Mr. Right or Mr. Wrong, can only do as much as we allow.

What are we showing that exemplifies who we are? What are our standards for ourselves? Do I dress the way I see myself, or the way I feel? Believe it or not, the way that a woman chooses to dress will tell a man a lot about her without her saying a word. What we do and how we carry ourselves define us and our true character. What we choose and accept ultimately makes us the women we become. Life is full of choices, but we must learn to choose wisely.

Hypothetically speaking, if you feel like you are not the woman that God has called and chosen you to be, or simply not the woman you desire to be, there is Great News! God can turn your life completely around if you allow him. He can break every chain of bondage on your life. He did it for me, and once you decide that you no longer want to settle for Mr. Wrong, he will do it for you! We do not become happy when we meet our mate we become happier. We should already love ourselves enough to be happy with ourselves. It's only when we find freedom in the way we think, freedom to believe, and freedom to love that we find true happiness. **Galatians 5:1 (KJV)** says: *"Stand fast therefore in the liberty wherewith Christ hath made us free, and be not entangled again with the yoke of bondage."*

In other words, God has made us free when we accepted him, so when he delivers you from a thing or a person, DON'T LOOK BACK! Come out of the slavery of settling and celebrate being single. It may be easier said than done, but its okay. You can do this. After all, to be free is worth it.

I know you're feeling great. Now, go on your date!

CHAPTER FOUR

The Dating Process

Congratulations! Let me be the first to say, "You look great!"

Are you asking yourself why am I saying this and you're only reading? Or you're probably saying I haven't even began the process. Here's where you stand corrected.

Yes, you have! You have already begun this process mentally. As you were reading, you were beginning to place yourself in a nice comfortable environment, alone, where it's nice and quiet. Yes, right there in your mind you gave yourself this makeover and I just had to be the first to say, well done!

Do you like the woman you have become? If so, your mental perception will and can soon transfer into your reality. I'm excited for you.

Grab the things you will need for the day you have planned ahead. Take only what's important. Plan to be alone for at least one hour. If you can handle more, take it. But here is the catch: when you arrive at your destination, leave your cell phone in the car. Your cell phone will serve as a distraction. Today, you will not have room for distractions. It's all about you, so make all necessary convo during the drive. Today is about loving yourself and getting to know yourself, alone. If right now you are saying, you're not going anywhere without your phone, that means you do not have time to spend with yourself. And if you don't want to be alone with you, who should? One hour without your phone will allow you to hear your innermost feelings about you.

Now it's time for your date. Your hair is fly, make-up on fleek, and you are dressed and looking classy. Let's go!

Ladies, when coming out of dead-wrong relationships and dead-end marriages, our biggest challenge is loving ourselves again totally. Of course you love you; you're you, and if no one else does, you have to love you. What I'm talking about is really learning to restore that energy that you once had before the break up or divorce. Heartbreak happens to the very best of us. Trust me, no woman is exempt. However, there are steps that we all should take in order to heal and begin loving ourselves again.

I chose to say this now because I know it's okay to do all the things that were mentioned in the previous chapter, like playing music to get your day started, taking the aroma therapeutic bubble bath with the scented candles, telling yourself you are beautiful, and etc. Here comes the hard part though. Taking yourself on the date.

Dating yourself can be rather tough but it is possible! Many times I would say, "I got this." I would go through all the necessary steps that you've learned, but as soon as I'd step out of the house I would get discouraged. To add insult to injury, once I reached my desired destination, the first couple I saw that appeared to be happy made me want to slap myself, like, *What are you trying to prove???* I would quickly have to remind myself of who I am and what my purpose was. I am beautiful, I am not settling and today I am taking myself out to prove to me that I can love me better than anyone.

Wherever your preference of location may be, make sure it is somewhere you can be comfortable so that you will not feel out of place. Your dating place may be the movie, the park, a local restaurant, or perhaps a local book store. You must go to a place that will make you happy. Now don't do what I first did after a break up. I decided to go see a movie, but not just any movie, a love story. Before I knew it I was in that theater bawling my eyes out, and therefore all the love I had given myself that day had dematerialized. I walked out feeling more hurt restored from what I had been through, than the happiness I was trying to gain from self-love. So please take my advice as you seek date destinations, go to places that give you confidence and keeps you strong.

You may also notice I never mentioned going to the mall or shopping as a date-yourself-experience. Negative! This is not an option. Especially for those of you who may already have a shopping addiction (such as I). I also tried this and it does not work. I will tell you why.

Retail therapy is equivalent to a temporary high. It only makes you feel good for the moment and then the thrill is gone. What generally happens in this situation is you will begin to spend money on unnecessary items as a way to compensate for lost affection. Going out buying new things is not a good way to prove that you really love yourself. You will do what is called, "reverse psychology" on yourself, trying to believe that if you spend money on you then you must love you. That is not the way to handle the dating process. So please ladies...do not do it. You only end up spending money on yourself as a pity party and not as a form of happiness. There is absolutely no reason to go broke because you are feeling inadequate. The best thing to do is accept where you are in life and make wise decisions for your day. The plan is to invest in a portion of your life (the dating process) not invest in your lifestyle (clothes, bags, and shoes, smile). You are special and very significant, and once you realize that, you will understand that you cannot put a label on something that's priceless. Of course this will be a challenge that you will only enjoy if you truly LOVE YOU!

Learning to save money should be a top priority while waiting on Mr. Right. We don't want to bring all beauty and no substance to a table, right ladies? We want a man to not only understand we are valuable, but *know* that we are valuable. Having your own shows a man that you care about your life more than your lifestyle, and that you're not broke and vulnerable looking to be saved when he arrives. Mr. Right wants "balance" just as much as he wants "beauty and brains." Building wealth while focusing on yourself is a sure way of practicing self-love and will assist Mr. Right in his selection as well.

How many of you know that a man has preferences, requirements, and standards for relationships as well? It does not matter if your finances are above, equivalent, or just below his. Mr. Right will never be intimidated by your education, employment, degrees, entrepreneurship, your hustle, or your skills because he understands that it's not a battle of the sexes, power struggles or competition. He's simply looking for Mrs. Right to compliment him.

Needless to say, you will get the hang of the dating process, how to build up your self-confidence and self-worth, as well as your finances while you wait. Although it may feel like you are walking through the fire waiting on Mr. Right, God will keep you! **Isaiah 58:11 (NLT)** says, *"The Lord will guide you always; he will satisfy your needs in a sun scorched land and will strengthen your frame, you will be like a well-watered garden, like a spring whose waters never fail."*

So you see, God's love never fails us. He has promised in his word that he will guide us and keep us satisfied, even when we are in what appears to be the driest places in our life. He has also promised to strengthen our bodies and to replenish us so that we will never thirst for a man. The worst place to be mentally for a single woman is emotionally thirsty. If you allow your spirit to become parched your physical body then becomes weak and vulnerable making it almost impossible to fight off temptation. Eat and drink off the word of God in this Season of your life that you may be able to sustain a level of boldness.

Just as it says in **Psalms 34:8 (KJV)** *"O taste and see that the Lord is good."*

I have great concern and confidence that your dating process is taking shape and that dating yourself was not all that bad. You should feel confident as well because it is now time to move on to another level. Move to a new level of love and respect for yourself. It is very simple. When you love yourself you make better decisions, and when you begin to make better decisions, you have mastered the technique of avoiding and settling for Mr. Wrong.

The benefit of learning to make better decisions is reaping the harvest that God has already prepared for you. There is someone out there that has been predestined to be your soul mate. I believe this to be true in your life as well as mine. So no matter how many bad relationships you have encountered it was all for your making. Always remember, what does not kill you will always make you stronger, and that was the purpose for some of the pain in your life. Things happen to get you to a place where you can learn to stop leaning on your own understanding and begin to totally trust God. **Proverbs 3:5 (KJV)** So, instead of always asking, why did this happen to me, the question should be, what can I learn from my past experiences? The only person that fails the same test over and over again are the ones that never study. God isn't sending you the same average Joe's in your life to intentionally trip you up or fail you. He's trying to open your eyes to your value and self-worth. He will permit the test, however, until your vision is no longer blurry but clear. With trust comes growth, with growth comes a level up.

To trust in God with our lives, destiny, and our mate means we are telling God, *I don't mind waiting on you and I believe your choice is better than mine. If this is the process that I have to go through in order to reap something better then I will trust that the blessing will be great. Not because I've been so good but because I know you're good.* God then begins to share himself with you and allow you to experience him on a more intimate level. He will give you the patience that you need to just wait. I've heard people say before, "Anything worth having at all is worth waiting on." I believe this is true.

The Bible says in **Ecclesiastes 9:11 (NLT)** "*I have observed something else under the sun. The fastest runner doesn't always win the race, and the strongest warrior doesn't always win the battle. The wise sometimes go hungry, and the skillful are not necessarily wealthy. And those who are educated don't always lead successful lives. It is all decided by chance, by being at the right place at the right time.*"

The anonymous writer of this book was simply saying, I have noticed that although we perceive things one way, it doesn't always mean they will happen as they appear. People don't always win because they are the best, wise doesn't mean you won't make mistakes, and being smart does not mean you will lead people in the right direction. However it's all about being lined up with the will and the word of God. New doors begin to open in your life when you allow God to work them out. If you avail yourself under the leadership and Godhead of the Father, he will make sure you are at the right place at the right time to receive your blessing. Always. Period.

Until then we have to work on building a lasting relationship with him, and learn to love ourselves past distraction and deceit. The dating process is the best way to get all of God and less of you. He will help you through this process if you will allow him. Again he does not step in and over power our decisions for his will. Whoever told you the myth of, "If God wants me to change, he will do it" lied to you. This attitude and way of thinking is a lie! God gives us all our own individual mindsets, and allows us to make our own conscious decisions. Change is a choice made by you, his guidance is a promise accepted by you. So in order to make a change you have to make sure that you are ready to turn away from what has so easily lead you astray. You have to trust that once he brings you out, you are out for good. No going back to broken relationships or abusive men. It's time to silence the settling once and for all. The only way you can do this successfully is get into his word for strength.

He said, *"If you abide in me, and my words abide in you, you shall ask what you will, and it shall be done to you"* **St. John 15:7 (KJV)**.

Ask for his strength during the dating process. Also, keep in mind never to be anxious for anything, just be patient, and see things through. Just because a man seems genuinely attracted to you does not mean he is the man God has for you. Ask God for a spirit of discernment to attach itself to you, that you may be able to distinguish a good spirit from a bad one. Everything that looks good doesn't always mean it's for you. We have to learn to pray that God will give us what we need and not what we want. What we want is not always what we need and what we need is the thing we often reject. Be wise as you wait for the Lord. His judgment is all you need!

I am excited about the breakthrough that's going to hit your life as you begin to walk in the things of God, trusting in him, leaning not on your own understanding, loving yourself completely through the process, controlling your thoughts while believing in yourself, celebrating being single and going on through the dating process! Now that you have conquered all these things let's accept his preparation.

CHAPTER FIVE

Accepting the Preparation

What are some of the things you would do if you were preparing for a test? Let's think in terms of a school test and compare how we prepare the way we learn in school to the way we should learn in relationships.

The way you prepare for a relationship has the same concept of approach of preparing to take a school test. There are things that must be done in order if you want to pass the test. You must never go to take a test without preparing yourself. The first thing you must understand is you have an assignment. How would you prepare for something you're not aware is coming? Therefore knowing you have an assignment is essential for the preparatory process.

The next thing you must do is study for the test. There are always key notes given or provided for the students to help them prepare for the test. After studying for the test, your next step is to focus on passing the test. While focusing on passing the test that means you have to bypass things that serve as distractions.

Dealing with Salvation, Dating, Relationships and Celibacy can be hard. You may be a woman that has never been married before and do not know the necessary steps for receiving Mr. Right. However, you have learned that it begins with YOU.

Let's say it together: "It begins with me!"

I want to share with you what God shared with me while I was in preparation.

We must understand that marriage is a covenant. It is a relationship ordained by God between two individuals. Once the two are joined together they become one, but with God it becomes a threefold cord that cannot be easily broken. However, we as women, have to be whole and complete within ourselves first.

What makes a woman whole and complete? I am glad you asked.

Number one: being able to forgive the ones that have offended you, hurt you, and caused you pain. Number two: You have to learn to live past the pain. Number three: You have to learn to love yourself enough to press towards the promise. (Please read **Philippians 3:14**)

Once you are able to completely accept what makes you whole and complete, you have to understand your assignment. There is a place that God desires for us to be before he gives us who he desires for us to have. He wants to bless us simply because he loves us, and it gives him no greater joy than to see his children happy. But there are stipulations to his giving.

His word says in **Matthew 6:33 (KJV)** *"But seek ye first the Kingdom of God and his righteousness; and all these things will be added unto you."*

What things? Whatsoever your heart desires is what he will grant unto you. The things that you have been praying and seeking his face for.   **Mark 11:24 (NIV)** says: *"Therefore I tell you, whatever you ask for in Prayer, believe that you have received it and it will be yours."*

Realistically speaking, would God give you a million dollar mansion on a ten dollar an hour mentality? No. So let's not pray amiss. Pray for things that you desire, not what you covet.

Our assignment is not to sit back and pray every night that God will send a husband into our lives. Sometimes we have to be careful what we pray and ask God for because if it is not our season to reap, when the enemy sends something that looks good, and talks a good game, we fall for the counterfeit rather than the promise. So, instead of being desperate and unfocused, our assignment is to seek the will and the face of God through Prayer. We have to pray that it is his will being done in our lives and not our own. We have to know, trust, and believe that he hears our prayers and that he will answer them. Listen for his voice so you will not be lead astray when the enemy or, again, the "inner me" (which is your own untamed desires) tries to set up traps.

How do you hear the voice of God? You hear the voice of God by listening in your quiet time with him.

Often times God is giving us answers to situations we have prayed about and because it does not feel comfortable to us, we do not receive it. What ultimately happens is we end up moving forward in relationships that God has not ordained. Then, nothing seems to work out right, we go through pure hell in the midst of it, and then spend so much time trying to gain back what was lost during our act of disobedience. There are a lot of things that are lost that we can get back, but time spent with Mr. Wrong is not one of them. Then we question God why he is not moving in our lives and why he allowed us to go through such a situation and he's saying, "I am moving in your life, you are not listening!"

God has a voice; he speaks in several different ways. He speaks to us through our Pastors to bring confirmation to our thoughts. He speaks through personal life situations when he allows things to happen contrary to our plans. He speaks to us through dreams. God is not limited; he will speak to us from a bumper sticker if he has to. We may not always understand what God is saying or why he may be saying it but we should always make sure we are listening.

I know the issues of life. Disappointments and having to have patience for what God has planned can be rather confusing. But I am lead to believe that it is all well worth the wait. Just think about it for a moment. If you are in a relationship right now that you know you need to be released from because it's causing you too much heartache and pain, and not enough happiness, then you are settling. But how much more pain do you think you can handle before you become burnt out and jaded in love? Or better yet, how much more patience are you willing to give just to wait on God to fulfill his promises in your life? When we get beside ourselves in our own selfish thinking, lusts, and desires, the process of God stops. We are then moving ahead of God. I know and surely understand that it can be challenging, frustrating and discouraging while waiting on Mr. Right, but after settling for Mr. Wrong for so long, eventually we give up the fight and choose the God/good way out.

Unfortunately there are women all over the world who will find themselves settling for Mr. Wrong everyday simply because they don't know who they are yet. They do not want to be alone. They do not have enough patience or they may not trust God. But I pray that this book will enlighten you and also minister to your spirit that you may consider another sister that may be going through so that she too may receive healing through these words and her very own belief. But now that you know who you are, and understand that your assignment is to do the will of God first; we can begin studying for the test.

In order to study for a test you must have your notes. Let's refer back to the quiz provided in the introduction. Did you pass the test? If not, then you will need to study what it takes to never settle for the wrong man again. Whatever area you have failed in as it relates to settling you have to make sure you stay away from that type of man. I know you may be saying that it just doesn't seem like there are any more good men out there. Well I want to assure you that there are still good men left. We must speak that in order to believe it. The problem is we've spent so much time settling for Mr. Wrong that we don't recognize Mr. Right when he comes. We've been hurt so many times by the men we thought were our Mr. Right that we have begun to put all men in the same box of "no good stuff" and toss them out. We literally give up the possibility of being happy with anyone, which leads to setbacks, failures, and settling.

We're afraid to trust God with this process and for our mate that we will often times give ourselves over and settle. We have to put an end to this reckless and careless behavior.

I want to share just a little bit of the story of Ruth in the Bible. I don't take lightly that all know the story, but if you have never read it, please do so. I believe it will bless you tremendously.

Ruth had a mother-in-law named Naomi. Naomi had two sons, one married Ruth, the other married Oprah. Both men died along with Naomi's husband, therefore, all of the women were widows. Naomi decided to leave the country where she was living and return home to her own people. Meanwhile, the ladies wanted to follow but against Naomi's will. She begged them to return to their own families, saying that she has no more sons to give them. Oprah finally agreed to leave, but Ruth remained at her side, telling her that wherever she ventured, there she would journey also. It showed the amount of love she had for Naomi, and many may wonder why she didn't go back to her own kin. I will be the first to say that sometimes you must understand that separating from what's familiar to you is necessary.

While it may have seemed strange to Naomi, as well as others around her that watched her straggling along behind Naomi, God saw it as humility and obedience. Naomi knew the loyalty that was within Ruth was great and God allowed her to instruct Ruth on what to do in order to receive a good man. The good man's name was Boaz! Because Ruth was obedient and in the right place at the right time she received Mr. Right! Not only was he wealthy, he had his own land and property! Can I get an Amen, ladies?

Let's reflect on what the word of God says for a moment. If *you* believe when you pray *you* shall receive. **Mark 11:24 (KJV)**

So, if you want God to send you a good man you have to pray prayers according to what you believe you are prepared to receive. If you received a man that does not treat you the way you want to be treated, he was not sent from God. Satan has a way of playing on your mind and its ability to think accurately after you have waited so long. His job is to wear out the patience of the saints. So naturally any man that comes along and tells you some nice things you want to hear, you may fall for it. This too is a form of settling. The Bible tells us to try the spirit by the spirit and see whether they are of God because many false prophets have went out into the world. **1 John 4:1 (KJV)** This means, "STUDY!" Do your homework! Don't accept the first thing flying because he looks and smells good because if his spirit isn't right with God then it will be impossible for him to treat you right.

A man that does not know how to treat a woman is not a complete man. There are holes in his life, in his story. There was something that went undone in his life. Maybe his father was not in his life as a good role model and example of how to treat a lady and the importance thereof. Maybe his father was a part of his life but all he witnessed was the abuse issued to his mother, or perhaps his father was present but conveniently unavailable. Meaning, he was in the household, but he wasn't a dad. You would be surprised at the number of men who had a father present but was never taught how to do simple things such as tie a suit tie. Truthfully, men need other men for support and guidance, but more importantly, they need God. How far do you think a man can lead you if he doesn't know where he is going?

"But let us not be weary in well doing for in due season we shall reap, if we faint not." **Galatians 6:9 (KJV)** I encourage you to hold on with great faith because your breakthrough is coming. God has someone special just for you!

Okay now back to the study guide. If you passed the test I would like to say congratulations. But let's say you failed the test by right at 50 points, and the men you've dated had issues such as: he's not saved, he's verbally and physically abusive, does not have a job, and borrows your money. There's a big problem. You must first learn to pass the test by going through the necessary steps in Chapters 1 through 4 to ensure yourself that you are, in fact, worthy of someone better. Once those things have been accomplished, you can begin trying to pass the test by creating a not-to-do-list. It is perfectly okay to make a list of do's and don'ts to help you figure out the type of man to stay away from as opposed to the type of man you would like to enter your life.

For example, I do not want a man who cheats. I do not want a man who lives with his mother. I do not want a man who never calls to see how I am doing. On the contrary, I do want a man with his own money. I do want a man with his own car. I do want a man with good credit. I do want a man who has his own home. I do want a man that's saved. Yes ladies, it is okay to want a man that is saved. Women have this preconceived notion that saved men are no fun. That is so not true. I believe that a saved man can be just as fun as a worldly man, and the great difference would be he loves the Lord with his whole heart. Saved is not stupid nor boring, it's a choice to live upright to the best of your ability. However, I believe everyone should have balance, which includes an active spiritual life as well as a fun social life with family and friends.

Always set your standards based upon what you have been through and the things you have experienced. I have heard so many men say women set their standards too high and that's why we are single. This is not true, so do not believe this. We actually set our standards based upon what we feel we deserve. Quite naturally if you have been going through the same things over and over again, you do not want to fall for the brother that you fell for in the past. So it's time to look past that brother and on to something better, which means that you have to level up a little bit higher and say, "I will do better next time because I deserve it!"

It is never okay to settle for someone who has no car, no money, no job, lives with his mama, has five and six kids or more floating around that he does not care for, borrows your money, never compliments you, never reaches out to you, and worst of all, beats on you. If you are with a man like this or have ever experienced this type of man, RUN FOR YOUR LIFE! He is not worth your time, and will only devalue you and lower your self- esteem. Learn to really trust and wait on God.

It may have come as a surprise to some of you that you did not pass the test. Others of you may have known you would fail. One of the reasons why we fail the test is because we do not like to study. Before going into a relationship it is critical that you get to know the person you are dealing with. How do you do this? By studying them. Ask questions about their life. Find out what his previous relationship was like. Has he ever been married before? If divorced, you should want to know honestly what caused it. Does he have children? If so, what is his relationship like with them? Find out how often does he see them and does he have the means to take care of them financially? If not, this is definitely a red flag! A man that cannot support his children cannot take care of you.

Find out what his relationship is like with his mother. If she is still living? How often do they talk? Does he visit her, and can he help her if she's in need? This is very important to know. Trust me on this, ladies. A man that does not love his mother will never love you.

Is he stable? Consistent with work? Most importantly, does he love the Lord?

We have to have discerning spirits. Remember the Bible says to try the spirit by the spirit to make sure it's of God. So never take a person's word for it because there are some imposters and phony baloney's out there whose only objective is to lead silly women astray that don't know who they are. Make sure you take the time to really get to know the individual. There is no promissory note that proves if he loves the Lord he will love you, but the chances of that relationship is greater than naught. A man must find something to love first outside of his mother and father and if he can learn to acknowledge and love the power that's higher than him, loving a woman from his soul is possible. That's why we should always pray and wait on God. But…Do not be deceived there are also men of God in high positions of leadership and authority that are not truthful to their call and will lead innocent women astray with no intention of relationship or marriage. Be Careful!

These are all very strong methods to live by while waiting on Mr. Right. You have to study your target. As I stated in chapter 3 learn to have the Bird's Eye view. Do not concern yourself of the things a man can do for you now, but instead think of it for longevity. What are the plans for the future? Is he someone you feel can cover you in the spirit, can he provide for you and ultimately can you see yourself with him for the rest of your life? The only way you will get these answers is to consider God. Never be too hasty to jump into relationships just because you feel vulnerable. Give any situation you are about to get into a massive amount of thought. Try not to over analyze everything a man says and does but definitely base your decision on his positive actions. When we are negative people who always dwell and look for the negative things in others, that's what we attract. Then we haphazardly end up in a situation that is beneath our standards. But when we know better we do better. I hope this study guide has helped you discover new ways to date without falling for Mr. Wrong ever again.

Remember, get to know your mate. How can you marry someone you haven't taken the time to study/learn? Well enough of that let's prepare for the test because Mr. Right is on the way.

Finally it's time to focus on passing the test. After this, your confidence should be restored to a new level. You should have a new mind frame and focused on being the type of woman that good saved men seek after. You now have the ability to say no to the approach of Mr. Wrong. The only way to accomplish this is to truly be praying for a good, God fearing man. If you have been dating men with no job then you of course want to say "NO" to the brother that says, "I don't work, but I get paid. As long as I handle my business I'm straight." Again, RUN!

The Bible says in **Thessalonians 3:10 (DBT)** *"If any man does not like to work, neither let him eat."* So if he does not work to provide, your job is not to feed him.

On the other hand, be careful of asking God for things you're unwilling to do for yourself. In other words, if you are not whole and complete within yourself and do not work before meeting the man, how much more can you expect to receive? There is a song that Lyfe Jennings wrote called "Statistics" and in this song he said, 'Don't be a nickel out here looking for a dime.'

Women, focus on you more than anything. Make it your purposeful duty to be the set standard that you set for Mr. Right. Set goals for your life and reach them. Always try to obtain things on your own that you will not need from a man. Again, you should be able to bring your own things to the table.

I think it is a man's top priority to compliment his woman on how good she looks. If he doesn't, then someone else will. Never settle for a man who does not have it in himself to tell you that you are beautiful. It is very well pleasing for a woman to feel like a Queen, which gives the Queen much more enthusiasm to take care of her King. So always expect the respect that comes from a King to a Queen and nothing less than that. We must remember to allow a man to always be a man; however it is quite okay to challenge his kindness. Allow him to do the pleasant things for you like open your car door, pull out your chair before you eat while dining out, and also rub your feet and your back. After all you've been through you deserve it. We gladly reciprocate the kindness to someone we feel are worthy of great things.

Now, let's focus on doing things that prepare us for the test. Learning the necessary things we should do as women will help us to prepare for Mr. Right.

For example, practicing cleanliness towards your home. This is a test every woman that wants a good man should pass. Cleanliness is next to Godliness, so if you are in Christ your temple should be clean (which is your body) as well as your home. Never get too caught up in today's work that you cannot tend to or maintain the upkeep of your home. A former pastor of mine would always say these words, "You have to stay ready to keep from getting ready." It has stuck with me for years and is also a major slogan I live by. Being a neat and clean person should always be a woman's top priority. This is not optional for certain purposes, it is a must. Keep your house in order by all means necessary. This is impressive to Mr. Right. Always be the type of woman that makes sure her home is in welcoming condition so you will never have to rush to get ready.

Are you a good cook? You say you want Mr. Right, don't you? Well, are you confident that you have what it takes to not only attract Mr. Right but to satisfy and keep him? Of course Mr. Right loves to eat, and nothing has changed. The way to a man's heart is still through his stomach. So, if by chance you do not know how to cook or feel you can cook, but you're not very good at it, learn how to cook! I'm laughing as I say this because I know there are some women out there that will say they don't know how to cook or have the time. However, McDonalds and Chic Fil A won't keep him at home. Besides, there are so many cook books available in stores everywhere. Just follow the directions and be great. (Smile) Remember, you are preparing yourself for Mr. Right so these are things that would be good to know. They're not always necessary, but very good to possess.

What do you have to offer Mr. Right when he comes? Will he be comfortable in your domain? Let me ask you this question: If God sent your husband to you this week would you be ready, or would you have to get prepared? A lot of us want to be married, but I think we get the false impression of what marriage is all about. Most women don't want to be married anymore once they find out what true marriage is all about, while others just want to be married to have sex. *News Flash* my sister, marriage is not just about having sex. If that were the case you could skip right over Chapters 1 through 4 and move directly to 5 and see how it works out without getting to know the person you marry. We have to make sure that if we want Mr. Right that we are not Mrs. Wrong. So we must know how to carry ourselves as ladies and never ever make a man feel like sex is more important than "true love." If you make the mistake of doing this you will miss the promises God has ordained for the covenant.

Let's talk about the standards of men. They do not want a woman that does not meet their standards. There are things that men love about women, and thankfully, it's not all about outside physicality or intimate pleasure. A man loves a lady that walks in the shoes of a woman. Someone who's classy, has a lot of respect for herself and others, has her own job, her own money, her own home and for the icing on the cake, able to cook and clean! Your curves are just a bonus! Don't think because your fine as wine and can shake your behind that a man won't leave for someone that is possibly less attractive, yet humble, modest, and can throw down in that kitchen!

Now there are some men out there who like the club girl, the one who hangs out all night, drinks, smokes, curses religiously, has multiple children, lives with her mother, does not work, and has no transportation. They like these women — but only for entertainment purposes. This type of woman will always have rocky relationships and will more than likely go from man to man, never stable, forever settling and too afraid to be alone to wait on God for Mr. Right. In her eyes he doesn't exist so she has made up her mind that her relationships will always fly by night and she is absolutely fine with this. At the end of the day, though, a real saved man is looking for a woman that has great strength and great potential. So let's then also learn to be the type of woman that men are looking to marry and not the type of woman he only wants to bed and clearly settles for.

Know your value and your worth. If you fall don't beat yourself up, simply know who you are. For every person that took advantage of your heart there is someone God will send to mend it. It will be their loss, so pray about it, get over it and move forward. Always tell yourself better is coming, and believe it. Don't get yourself together; keep yourself together because you never know when he is coming. Your blessing that you have been praying and seeking God for could be right around the corner from your house. Don't miss your breakthrough and your divine moment with Mr. Right because you're Mrs. Wrong. You are the key God has used to unlock doors to life. I don't know about you but that by far is enough to convince me that if God counted us worthy to be chosen for such a task, we are very special and should be treated nothing less than that.

IN CONCLUSION...

My prayer is that this book has left an impression on your heart that will last until the right man comes along, and that God himself would have ordained the connection and that you will know it is him. I pray that you will take these words of wisdom and inspiration and apply them to your life and encourage someone to read this book as well. There are millions of women that are dying all across the world because of brokenness and depression from abuse by the wrong men. Some women have even lost their lives because they thought they were entertaining someone who truly loved them. Do not let Satan set his traps in your life anymore. YOU DESERVE BETTER!

Be the woman God is calling you to be! Be independent in your own right. Have Faith but also learn to have patience. *"No good thing will the Lord uphold from them who walk uprightly."* **Psalms 84:11(KJV)** He is coming! Control your thoughts, believe in yourself, celebrate being single, learn to let go of the past, learn to forgive, go through the dating process alone, and accept the preparation while waiting on your mate!

And once you have learned to, "just wait for Mr. Right" and stay away from Mr. Wrong, you will then attract Greatness to your life!

Stop Settling Sis and Wait for Mr. Right! I pray you have been blessed!

Stop Settling Sis... Just Wait for Mr. Right

Made in the USA
Columbia, SC
16 June 2021